CHRISTMAS AT HOME
Holiday Party Pleasers

© 2010 by Barbour Publishing, Inc.

Compiled by Joanna Bloss.

ISBN 978-1-60260-972-3

Published by Barbour Publishing, Inc., P.O. Box 719, Uhrichsville, Ohio 44683, www.barbourbooks.com

Our mission is to publish and distribute inspirational products offering exceptional value and biblical encouragement to the masses.

 Member of the
Evangelical Christian
Publishers Association

Printed in China.

CHRISTMAS AT HOME
Holiday Party Pleasers

BARBOUR
PUBLISHING

CONTENTS

AROUND THE PUNCH BOWL: BEVERAGES

The best of all gifts around any Christmas tree:
the presence of a happy family all wrapped up in each other.

BURTON HILLIS

TRIPLE CHOCOLATE-MINT COCOA MIX

6 cups nonfat milk powder
1 (16 ounce) package powdered sugar
2 (8 ounce) jars chocolate-flavored nondairy powdered creamer
1 (7.5 ounce) package round peppermint candies, finely ground
¼ cup unsweetened cocoa powder
1 teaspoon salt

Combine all ingredients in very large bowl. To serve, pour 6 ounces boiling water over 3 tablespoons cocoa mix; stir until well blended. Store mix in airtight container in refrigerator.

SPICED TEA MIX

2 cups orange powdered drink mix
1 cup lemonade powdered drink mix
2 cups sugar
1 cup instant tea
1½ teaspoons cinnamon
¾ teaspoon ground cloves
½ cup red hot candies

Combine all ingredients in large bowl. To serve, pour 6 ounces boiling water over 4 teaspoons mix, stirring until well blended. Store mix in airtight container.

MULLED HOLIDAY PUNCH

1 quart apple juice
¼ cup brown sugar
2 cinnamon sticks
1 lemon, sliced
2 cups cranberry juice cocktail
½ teaspoon whole cloves

Combine all ingredients in large saucepan and simmer 15 minutes.
Serve hot.

HAWAIIAN LEMONADE PUNCH

1 (12 ounce) can frozen lemonade, thawed, plus one can water
3 cups apricot nectar, chilled
3 cups pineapple juice, chilled
1 (2 liter) bottle ginger ale

Combine thawed lemonade, apricot nectar, and pineapple juice. Add 1 can water. Add ginger ale right before serving.

WASSAIL

10 to 12 whole cloves
1 large orange
1 gallon apple cider
10 whole allspice
4 sticks cinnamon
1 cup brown sugar

Place whole cloves in rind of orange and heat in 275-degree oven for 1 hour. Bring cider to boil; add whole allspice and cinnamon. Boil 5 minutes; add brown sugar and boil 5 more minutes. Strain to serve. Float orange mixture in slow cooker or on top of stove on warm setting.

SPARKLING CRANBERRY PUNCH

2 quarts cranberry juice cocktail
1 (32 ounce) bottle sparkling water
1 cup (6 ounces) frozen pink lemonade

Chill cranberry juice and sparkling water. Thaw pink lemonade. Mix juice and lemonade in punch bowl. Stir in sparkling water just before serving.

DREAMSICLE PUNCH

1 (2 liter) bottle ginger ale
1 (12 ounce) can frozen orange juice concentrate
1 (24 ounce) can pineapple juice
1 orange, sliced for garnish
½ gallon orange sherbet
2 trays ice cubes

Mix ingredients together very carefully in large punch bowl. Add ice cubes last.

STRAWBERRY PUNCH

1 large package strawberry-flavored gelatin mix
2 cups boiling water
1 (12 ounce) can frozen lemonade
1 (12 ounce) can frozen orange juice
1 (46 ounce) can pineapple juice
2 quarts water
1 quart ginger ale

Dissolve gelatin mix in boiling water. Add frozen lemonade, frozen orange juice, pineapple juice, and water. Chill. Add ginger ale before serving. Yield: 40 (½ cup) servings

HOT CRANBERRY CIDER

1 quart apple juice or cider
1 (32 ounce) can cranberry juice
½ cup lemon juice
⅓ cup light brown sugar
8 whole cloves
2 cinnamon sticks

Boil all ingredients for 10 minutes and remove spices. Let simmer as guests help themselves.

FRUIT SLUSH

1¾ cups sugar
2 cups boiling water
1 (6 ounce) can frozen orange juice
3 cups apricot nectar
6 bananas, mashed
1 (20 ounce) can pineapple juice
1 (16 ounce) box frozen strawberries with juice

Dissolve sugar in boiling water. Stir in remaining ingredients and freeze.
Set out 2 to 3 hours before serving.

BEFORE THE CELEBRATION BEGINS:
BREAKFAST

I heard the bells on Christmas Day,
Their old, familiar carols play,
And wild and sweet
The words repeat
Of peace on earth, good-will to men!

HENRY WADSWORTH LONGFELLOW

APPLE CINNAMON FRENCH TOAST SOUFFLÉ

1 large loaf french bread
8 extra large eggs
3½ cups milk
½ cup sugar
1 tablespoon vanilla
6 to 8 medium Macintosh apples, peeled, cored, and sliced

Topping:
½ cup sugar
3 teaspoons cinnamon
1 teaspoon nutmeg
3 tablespoons butter

Preheat oven to 350 degrees. Spray 9x13-inch glass pan with cooking spray. Cut french bread into 1½-inch slices. Place bread tightly in pan. Combine eggs, milk, ½ cup sugar, and vanilla. Beat with whisk. Pour half of mixture over apples. Sprinkle topping over top. Dot with butter. Cover and chill overnight. Uncover and bake 60 to 75 minutes. Let rest 10 minutes. Serve with hot maple syrup and breakfast meat.

ARTICHOKE QUICHE

2 (6 ounce) jars marinated artichokes, chopped
1 small onion, chopped
1 clove garlic, minced
4 large eggs
¼ cup bread crumbs
¼ teaspoon salt
⅛ teaspoon pepper

⅛ teaspoon oregano
⅛ teaspoon hot pepper sauce
2 cups sharp cheddar cheese, grated
2 tablespoons fresh parsley, chopped
1 (9-inch) pie shell, unbaked

Preheat oven to 325 degrees. Drain artichokes and reserve marinade. Sauté onion and garlic in marinade and set aside. In large bowl, beat eggs and add bread crumbs, salt, pepper, oregano, and hot pepper sauce. Stir in cheese, parsley, chopped artichokes, and sautéed onion mixture. Pour into pie shell and bake 45 minutes or until done. Let stand 10 minutes before serving.

BREAKFAST PIE

1 pound sausage, cooked and crumbled
1½ cups Swiss cheese, shredded
1 (9-inch) pie shell, unbaked
¼ cup green bell pepper, chopped
¼ cup red bell pepper, chopped
2 tablespoons onion, chopped
4 eggs, lightly beaten
1 cup light cream

Preheat oven to 375 degrees. Mix sausage and cheese together and sprinkle into pie shell. Mix remaining ingredients together and pour over sausage/cheese mixture. Bake 40 to 45 minutes or until center is set. Cool 10 minutes before serving.

MAKE AHEAD MINI-QUICHES

1 package (12 rolls) butter flake dinner rolls
4½ ounces shrimp, drained
1 egg, beaten
½ cup half-and-half

½ teaspoon salt
Dash pepper
1⅓ cups Gruyere
cheese

Preheat oven to 375 degrees. Grease 2 dozen 1¾-inch muffin pans. Separate each dinner roll in half and press into the muffin pans to make the shells. Evenly distribute the shrimp in shells. Combine egg, cream, salt, and pepper. Divide this among the shells using approximately 2 teaspoons for each shell. Slice the cheese into 24 small triangles and place on top of each quiche. Bake 20 minutes. Serve immediately or cool and wrap in foil and freeze. To serve, place frozen appetizer on a baking sheet and bake for 10 to 12 minutes at 375 degrees.

EGGS FLORENTINE

9 eggs
1 pint cottage cheese
8 ounces Swiss cheese, grated
8 ounces feta cheese, cubed
4 tablespoons butter, softened
2 (10 ounce) packages frozen, chopped spinach, thawed and well-drained
1 teaspoon nutmeg

Preheat oven to 350 degrees. Beat eggs slightly. Add cheeses and butter and mix well. Stir in spinach and nutmeg. Pour into a greased 9x13-inch casserole. Bake 1 hour, or until knife inserted in center comes out clean.

CHRISTMAS MORNING BREAKFAST

16 slices white bread, crusts trimmed
1 (10 ounce) package Swiss cheese, cubed
2½ cups ham steak, cubed
4 eggs
3 cups milk
½ teaspoon dry mustard
½ teaspoon salt
2 cups cornflakes, crushed
½ cup butter, melted

Preheat oven to 350 degrees. Grease 9x13-inch pan and place 8 slices of bread on bottom. Spread cubed cheese and ham over bread. Place additional 8 slices of bread on top. Beat together eggs, milk, mustard, and salt. Pour over bread. Cover with foil and refrigerate overnight. Before baking, mix butter and cornflakes and spread over top of egg mixture. Bake uncovered 1 hour.

DUTCH BABIES

2 tablespoons butter
3 eggs, beaten
½ cup milk
½ cup flour

Preheat oven to 400 degrees. Melt butter in omelet pan or small round cake pan in hot oven. Combine beaten eggs, milk, and flour. Beat until fairly smooth. Pour batter into hot melted butter. Bake 15 minutes. Serve with syrup or fruit.

DELICIOUS EGG CASSEROLE

7 slices bread, cubed
1 pound sausage, cooked
1 cup cheese, grated
4 eggs
2 cups milk
½ teaspoon dry mustard
½ teaspoon salt
¼ teaspoon pepper
1 can cream of mushroom soup

Preheat oven to 325 degrees. In a 9x13-inch greased pan, layer bread, sausage, and cheese. Mix egg, milk, mustard, salt, and pepper. Pour over layered ingredients. Lightly press into bread with a rubber spatula. Pour cream of mushroom soup over the top. Cover and refrigerate at least 6 to 8 hours before baking. Bake about 35 minutes or until set.

FRENCH TOAST SUPREME

½ cup butter
2 tablespoons white corn syrup
1 cup brown sugar
French bread or Texas toast, sliced
5 eggs

1 (12 ounce) can
  evaporated milk
1 teaspoon vanilla
¼ teaspoon salt

In a small saucepan, heat butter, corn syrup, and brown sugar; boil for 1 minute. Spray 9x13-inch dish with cooking spray. Pour caramel mixture evenly on bottom. Place bread slices close together on top of caramel. Beat together eggs, evaporated milk, vanilla, and salt. Pour over top of bread, coating well. Cover with foil and refrigerate overnight. Bake at 350 degrees for 30 minutes, covered. Remove foil and bake 10 minutes more. When ready to serve, turn pieces over so caramel is on top.

BREAKFAST CASSEROLE

1 large loaf cinnamon bread, cut into 1-inch squares
1 (8 ounce) package cream cheese
1 dozen eggs
1 cup milk or sour cream
½ cup syrup

Place bread cubes in greased 9x13-inch dish. Blend cream cheese, eggs, milk, and syrup together. Pour over bread. Refrigerate overnight. Bake at 350 degrees for approximately 40 minutes or until knife comes out clean.

EGG TACOS

1 pound pork sausage
1 dozen eggs
8 ounces shredded cheese
Salsa
Taco shells

Brown sausage and drain well. Scramble eggs, being careful not to overcook. Add cheese, salsa, and sausage to the eggs. Fill shells with egg mixture.

NO-KNEAD CINNAMON ROLLS

Dough:
½ cup sugar
1 teaspoon salt
¼ cup butter, softened
¾ cup boiling water
¾ cup cold water
1 egg, beaten
1 package dry yeast
½ cup warm water
5½ cups flour

Filling:
¼ to ½ cup butter,
    softened
½ cup sugar
1 tablespoon cinnamon

Glaze:
¾ cup powdered sugar
½ teaspoon vanilla
1 tablespoon milk

Prepare dough: in a large mixing bowl combine sugar, salt, and butter. Pour ¾ cup boiling water over mixture and stir well. Add ¾ cup cold water. Add beaten egg. Dissolve yeast with ½ cup warm water and add to egg mixture. Stir in flour. Place in greased bowl and cover with a cloth. Let rise in warm place 2½ hours.

Prepare rolls by rolling dough on floured surface into a 24x12-inch rectangle. Evenly spread softened butter across rectangle. Mix sugar and cinnamon together and sprinkle over butter-covered dough. Starting at the longest end, tightly roll dough, pinching ends to seal. Slice dough into 1- to 1½-inch portions and place 12 rolls each in 2 greased 9x13-inch pans. Cover with cloth and let rise in warm place for 1½ hours.

Bake at 350 degrees for 17 to 20 minutes, being careful not to overbake. Let rolls cool slightly in pan. While cooling, mix glaze ingredients and spread over warm rolls.

BUTTERSCOTCH BUBBLE BREAD

1 cup pecans, chopped, divided
1 package frozen rolls (24)
1 package butterscotch pudding mix (not instant)
1 cup brown sugar
Cinnamon
½ cup butter

Distribute half of the pecans in bottom of Bundt pan. Spread the rolls out evenly in bottom. Sprinkle dry pudding mix over rolls, then sprinkle rest of nuts. Sprinkle brown sugar and cinnamon on top then slice stick of butter on top. Cover and let rise 8 to10 hours (overnight). Bake at 350 degrees for 25 minutes. Turn out while hot.

GETTING THE FESTIVITIES STARTED: APPETIZERS

At Christmas play and make good cheer,
For Christmas comes but once a year.

THOMAS TUSSER

CREAMY AVOCADO DIP

2 large avocados
½ cup medium salsa
1½ cups Monterey Jack cheese, grated
6 green onions
1½ cups cheddar cheese, grated
1½ cups sour cream
1 to 2 tomatoes, chopped

Using an 8x10-inch serving dish, layer ingredients in order given. Serve with tortilla chips.

ARTICHOKE DIP

1 (15 ounce) can artichoke hearts, drained and chopped fine
1 cup mozzarella cheese
1 cup mayonnaise
1 cup Parmesan cheese
Paprika
Garlic salt

Preheat oven to 350 degrees. Mix all ingredients together and place in greased casserole dish. Sprinkle with paprika and garlic salt to taste. Bake 25 to 30 minutes.

HOT CRAB DIP

2 (8 ounce) packages cream cheese
1 (8 ounce) carton sour cream
4 tablespoons mayonnaise
½ teaspoon lemon juice
1 teaspoon dry mustard

1 cup cheddar cheese,
  shredded
Dash onion salt
Dash paprika
1 pound crab

Preheat oven to 325 degrees. Mix all ingredients except crab and ⅓ cup cheese in food processor. Fold in crab. Put ⅓ cup cheese on top. Bake 30 to 40 minutes.

HUMMUS

2 (16 ounce) cans chickpeas
3 cloves garlic, minced
6 tablespoons tahini
6 tablespoons lemon juice

Handful parsley, chopped
½ teaspoon salt
½ teaspoon cumin
Olive oil

Mash chickpeas. Add garlic, tahini, lemon juice, parsley, salt, and cumin. Moisten with olive oil. Serve on pita bread and crackers.

HOLIDAY DIP

1 (8 ounce) package cream cheese
3 tablespoons mayonnaise
2 tablespoons milk
½ onion, sautéed
½ red pepper, chopped
½ green pepper, chopped
½ pound bacon, fried and crumbled
1 cup sour cream

Preheat oven to 350 degrees. Combine all ingredients and spread into a 10-inch glass pie dish. Bake 20 to 30 minutes. Serve with favorite crackers.

BAKED BRIE

1 sheet puff pastry, thawed
¼ cup pecans or walnuts, chopped
⅛ cup raspberry or apricot jam
1 (17 ounce) package Brie cheese
1 egg, well beaten

Preheat oven to 375 degrees. Unfold pastry sheet onto floured board. Roll out gently. Spread nuts and jam in center of sheet, forming a circle the size of the Brie, completely covering it. Place Brie on top. Fold sides of pastry up and around Brie, completely covering it. Trim off excess. Turn Brie over onto pie plate or shallow baking dish. Cut decorations out of the excess pastry and set aside. Brush beaten egg over top and sides of Brie. Decorate with pastry shapes. Brush again with egg. Bake for 30 minutes. Let stand for 30 minutes. Serve with water crackers.

CHEESE BLINTZ APPETIZER

2 (8 ounce) packages cream cheese
2 egg yolks
½ cup sugar
1 teaspoon lemon juice
2 loaves white bread with crust removed
1 cup butter, melted
1 cup brown sugar
3 teaspoons cinnamon

Blend cream cheese, egg yolks, sugar, and lemon juice. Flatten sliced bread and spread each slice with the cheese mixture. Roll up and dip each roll into melted butter, then into brown sugar and cinnamon mixture. Freeze for at least 3 hours until ready to bake. Cut each roll into thirds. Bake on ungreased cookie sheet, seam side down, 15 to 20 minutes at 350 degrees.

MARINATED MOZZARELLA

1 pound mozzarella cheese, cut into bite-size cubes
2 cups olive oil
½ teaspoon thyme
1 teaspoon oregano
1½ teaspoons dried parsley
3 cloves garlic, minced
¼ teaspoon paprika
½ teaspoon dried pepper flakes

Combine all ingredients in a 1-quart glass jar. Cover and shake to blend. To marinate, allow to set at room temperature for 5 days, shaking jar daily. Store at room temperature.

VEGETABLE PIZZA

2 packages crescent rolls
¼ cup onion, chopped
¾ cup mayonnaise
¼ cup sour cream (or half-and-half)
2 (8 ounce) packages cream cheese
½ teaspoon garlic powder
1 teaspoon dill weed
Choice of fresh vegetables (broccoli, cauliflower, tomatoes, shredded carrots, black olives, etc.)

Flatten crescent rolls on large cookie sheet. Bake according to directions, until golden brown. Cool. Mix onion, mayonnaise, sour cream, cream cheese, garlic powder, and dill weed. Spread mixture over crust. On top, sprinkle finely sliced vegetables.

EASY CHEESE BALL

1 (8 ounce) package cream cheese
1 cup ham, finely minced
½ teaspoon horseradish
1 tablespoon sour cream
1 cup cheddar jack cheese, shredded
Walnuts

Let cream cheese sit out for 1 hour. Combine cream cheese, ham, horseradish, and sour cream in mixer. Add shredded cheese. Freeze 15 minutes. Form into a ball. Roll in walnuts. Refrigerate 1 to 2 hours or until ready to serve. Good with crackers, pretzels, or vegetables.

NO FAIL PARTY DIP

1 (15 ounce) can chili without beans
4 ounces cream cheese
½ cup onion, chopped
2 cups cheddar jack cheese, shredded, divided

In 1-quart glass bowl, combine chili, cream cheese, onion, and 1 cup shredded cheese. Cover and microwave for 2 minutes and stir until blended. Top with remaining cheese and microwave 1 minute without stirring. Serve hot with tortilla chips.

PARTY TURNOVERS

1 pound ground beef
1 teaspoon salt
½ teaspoon pepper
2 tablespoons onion, minced
½ clove garlic, finely minced
1 cup cheddar cheese, shredded
3 (8 ounce) tubes crescent rolls

Preheat oven to 375 degrees. In medium skillet, brown hamburger with salt, pepper, onion, and garlic. Drain. Stir in cheese. Separate crescent dough. Place a tablespoonful of meat mixture in center of each triangle, fold over, and seal edges. Place on ungreased baking sheet and bake for 15 minutes or until golden brown.

GREEN, WHITE, AND RED LAYERED DIP

1 (16 ounce) container sour cream
½ cup mayonnaise
½ cup ranch dressing
1 medium ripe avocado, peeled and mashed
2 tablespoons cilantro, chopped
½ cup roasted red peppers, finely chopped
½ teaspoon paprika

Mix sour cream, mayonnaise, and ranch dressing. Divide into 3 portions, about 1 cup each. Mix 1 portion with avocado and cilantro. Stir in red peppers and paprika into second portion; leave third portion plain. Spoon portions into shallow bowl or pie plate; cover. Refrigerate several hours or until chilled. Serve with tortilla chips and assorted cut-up vegetables.

SPICED NUTS

1 teaspoon chili powder
½ teaspoon cinnamon
4 cups unsalted mixed nuts
4 tablespoons unsalted butter

6 tablespoons brown sugar
1 tablespoon water
1 teaspoon salt

Mix spices and set aside. Heat nuts in dry skillet and cook, stirring frequently until they begin to toast (about 4 minutes). Add butter and cook, stirring until nuts begin to darken (about 1 minute). Add spices, brown sugar, water, and salt; cook, stirring until sauce thickens and nuts are glazed (about 5 minutes). Remove nuts from heat and transfer to baking sheet lined with aluminum foil, separating them with a fork. Let nuts stand until cooled and sugar has hardened, about 10 minutes. Store in an airtight container.

ONION DIP

3 medium onions, 2 unpeeled, 1 peeled
1 cup olive oil
1 cup mayonnaise
1 cup sour cream
1 tablespoon white wine vinegar
2 teaspoons salt
2 scallions (white and green parts), minced
Freshly ground black pepper
Hot pepper sauce

Preheat oven to 425 degrees. Rub unpeeled onions with a bit of olive oil; roast until soft, about 45 minutes. Cool and peel. Finely dice peeled raw onion. Heat large skillet over medium-high heat; add remaining oil and heat until quite hot. Add diced onion and cook, stirring occasionally, until edges begin to brown, about 5 minutes. Turn to medium-low and cook until onion is golden brown, about 18 minutes. Scrape onion, oil, and juices into a sieve over a bowl. Drain onions and spread on a paper towel–lined plate. Cool strained oil. Puree roasted onions in food processor. Add mayonnaise, sour cream, vinegar, and salt; pulse until smooth. With motor running, drizzle in ¼ cup of the flavored reserved oil. Transfer to serving bowl. Stir in scallions, pepper, and hot sauce to taste. Refrigerate at least 3 hours. Scatter fried onions over top just before serving with potato chips.

CHIPOTLE CHICKEN CUPS

36 wonton wrappers
Cooking spray
1½ cups sharp cheddar cheese, shredded
1 cup cooked chicken, chopped
1 cup roasted red bell peppers, chopped
1 cup chipotle salsa
½ cup green onions, chopped

Preheat oven to 350 degrees. Fit 1 wonton wrapper into each of 36 mini muffin cups coated with cooking spray, pressing the wrappers into sides of cups. Bake for 7 minutes or until lightly browned. Keep wontons in muffin cups. Combine cheese and remaining ingredients, and spoon about 1 tablespoon cheese mixture into each wonton cup. Bake 6 minutes or until cheese melts. Remove from muffin cups. Serve immediately.

SIMPLE FRUIT DIP

1 (8 ounce) package cream cheese, softened
¾ cup brown sugar
¼ cup sugar
1 teaspoon vanilla

Combine all ingredients in a small mixing bowl. Blend thoroughly with electric mixer. Transfer to a pretty serving dish and serve with sliced fruit, such as bananas, apples, grapes, or strawberries.

ALMOND CHEDDAR APPETIZERS

1 cup mayonnaise
2 teaspoons Worcestershire sauce
1 cup sharp cheddar cheese, shredded
1 medium onion, chopped
¾ cup slivered almonds, chopped
6 bacon strips, cooked and crumbled
1 loaf (1 pound) french bread

Preheat oven to 400 degrees. In a bowl, combine the mayonnaise and Worcestershire sauce; stir in cheese, onion, almonds, and bacon. Cut bread into ½-inch slices; spread with cheese mixture. Cut slices in half. Place on greased baking sheet. Bake 8 to 10 minutes or until bubbly. Makes 4 dozen.

MINI MEATBALLS

1 pound ground beef
1 teaspoon salt
1 teaspoon basil
Dash pepper
1 (32 ounce) jar spaghetti sauce

Mix meat and spices; shape into small meatballs. Brown in small amount of shortening. Heat spaghetti sauce and add browned meatballs to sauce. Serve warm as appetizers.

LIGHT & TASTY:
SOUPS AND SALADS

*Glory to God in the highest, and on earth
peace to men on whom his favor rests.*

LUKE 2:14 NIV

WINTER MINESTRONE

1 tablespoon olive oil
1 clove garlic, minced
1 medium onion, coarsely chopped
1 cup potato, diced
½ cup celery, chopped
½ carrot, sliced
1 cup cabbage, shredded
1 (8 ounce) can chopped tomatoes in juice
1 (15½ ounce) can kidney beans
1 cup beef or chicken broth
¼ cup fresh parsley, chopped
¼ cup fresh basil, chopped
Pepper to taste
½ cup small dry pasta
Parmesan cheese

Combine oil, garlic, and onion in a 2-quart, microwave-safe casserole dish. Cover with lid. Microwave on high for 1 minute. Add potato, celery, carrot, and cabbage. Drain juice from tomatoes into casserole dish. Cover again and microwave on high until vegetables are tender, 6 to 8 minutes. Add tomatoes, beans, broth, parsley, basil, and pepper. Cover again and microwave on high until heated through, 8 to 10 minutes. Meanwhile, cook pasta in 2 cups boiling water on stove, according to package directions. Drain pasta and pour into soup at end of cooking time. Sprinkle with Parmesan cheese before serving.

SHRIMP BISQUE

6 tablespoons butter
4 tablespoons green pepper,
   finely chopped
4 tablespoons onion,
   finely chopped
1 scallion, chopped
2 tablespoons parsley, chopped
1½ cups fresh mushrooms, sliced

2 tablespoons flour
1 cup milk
1 teaspoon salt
½ teaspoon white pepper
Dash hot sauce
1½ cups half-and-half
1½ cups shrimp,
   cooked and drained

Heat 4 tablespoons butter in a skillet; add green pepper, onion, scallion, parsley, and mushrooms and sauté until soft (about 5 minutes). In a saucepan, heat remaining 2 tablespoons butter; stir in flour. Add milk; cook, stirring until thickened and smooth. Stir in salt, pepper, and hot sauce. Add sautéed vegetables and half-and-half. Bring to boil, stirring; reduce heat. Add shrimp and simmer uncovered for 5 minutes.

CARROT SOUP

¼ cup butter
1 pound carrots, peeled and sliced
1 stick celery, chopped
1 large potato, diced
1 medium onion, chopped
4 cups chicken broth

Melt butter in large frying pan. Sauté carrots, celery, potato, and onion in butter for 15 minutes. Add broth and cook for 15 more minutes. Cool and pass through blender.

PUMPKIN APPLE SOUP

1 or 2 tablespoons butter
1 medium onion, chopped (about ½ cup)
1 clove garlic, minced
3 cups canned chicken broth
1 (16 ounce) can pumpkin
1 tablespoon sugar
¼ teaspoon cinnamon
2 Granny Smith apples, peeled and coarsely chopped
1 cup heavy cream

Melt butter in a soup pot. Add onion and garlic. Cook until tender, but not brown, 3 to 4 minutes. Stir in broth, pumpkin, sugar, and cinnamon. Add apples. Heat until boiling. Cover. Reduce heat and simmer 10 minutes. Add cream. Puree in batches in blender or food processor. Return to pot to heat through. Season to taste with salt and pepper. Makes approximately 6 to 8 servings.

CLAM CHOWDER

6 slices bacon
1 cup onion, diced
2 (6½ ounce) cans minced clams,
 drained (reserve juice)
1 (8 ounce) can clam juice
 or 8 ounces water

3 cups pared, diced potatoes
4 tablespoons flour
3 cups milk
Salt and pepper to taste

In a large soup pot, gently fry bacon until crisp. Remove with slotted spoon and drain on paper towel. Add diced onion to pot and bacon drippings; sauté until golden brown. Remove onion and set aside. Pour off as much grease from pot as possible, then pour in drained clam juice, clam juice or water, and potatoes. Boil gently, covered, until potatoes are done. Gradually add milk to flour and whip until smooth. Add flour mixture, remaining milk, and drained clams to the pot. Cook gently until thickened, stirring constantly. Add reserved onion and bacon.

WHITE "CHRISTMAS" CHILI

3 teaspoons olive oil
2 large onions, thinly sliced
1 clove garlic, minced
2 cups chicken broth
1 cup white grape juice
2 (15½ ounce) cans cannellini beans, drained and rinsed
¼ cup fresh-squeezed lime juice
1 (4 ounce) can green chilies, chopped
1 jalapeño pepper, stemmed, seeded, and minced
4 tablespoons fresh cilantro, minced
1 teaspoon oregano, dried
½ teaspoon cumin
¼ teaspoon cinnamon
3 cups smoked whole turkey, shredded
1 cup Monterey Jack cheese

Pour oil in a pan and place over medium-high heat. Sauté onions and garlic, stirring until onions are golden and taste sweet, about 20 minutes. Add 2 cups of broth, white grape juice, beans, lime juice, green chilies, jalapeños, cilantro, oregano, cumin, and cinnamon. Bring to boil over high heat; cover and simmer 15 minutes. Stir in shredded turkey and cheese. When chili is hot, ladle into bowls and add diced tomatoes and/or fresh cilantro leaves.

GAZPACHO

1½ pounds fresh tomatoes
2 green bell peppers
2 red bell peppers
1 hard-boiled egg
2 garlic cloves
2 slices dry white bread
2 cups croutons
1½ cups tomato juice
3 tablespoons extra virgin olive oil
2 tablespoons sherry vinegar
Salt
Fresh ground black pepper
1 tray ice cubes (8 to 12)

Peel and remove seeds from tomatoes and chop into small pieces. Chop green and red peppers and egg into small cubes. Peel and chop garlic cloves. Remove crust from the dry white bread and break into small pieces. Place chopped tomatoes, garlic, white bread, croutons, tomato juice, olive oil, and sherry vinegar together with half of the green and red bell peppers into blender or food processor with ice. Blend until smooth. Add salt and black pepper, according to taste. Pour contents through a fine nylon or steel strainer.

FROZEN SALAD

1 (8 ounce) package cream cheese
¾ cup sugar
1 (10 ounce) package frozen strawberries and juice
1 (20 ounce) can crushed pineapple, drained
2 bananas
1 tablespoon lemon juice
1 (8 ounce) container whipped topping

Cream together cream cheese and sugar. Add in order: strawberries, juice, pineapple, bananas, and lemon juice. Fold in whipped topping. Freeze.

CHERRY SALAD

1 (16 ounce) can cherry pie filling
1 (8 ounce) can crushed pineapple, drained
1 cup miniature marshmallows
½ cup coconut
½ cup pecans, chopped
1 (15 ounce) can sweetened condensed milk
1 (9 ounce) container nondairy whipped topping

Mix together cherry pie filling, pineapple, marshmallows, coconut, pecans, and sweetened condensed milk. Fold in whipped topping. Refrigerate or freeze until ready to serve.

APPLE SALAD

1 red delicious apple, cubed
1 golden delicious apple, cubed
½ cup seedless raisins
½ cup seedless golden raisins
½ cup raw celery, diced

¼ cup walnuts, chopped
1 orange, juiced
1 (8 ounce) carton
    vanilla yogurt
Cinnamon

In medium bowl, combine apples, raisins, celery, and nuts. Blend juice from orange into yogurt and pour over fruit mixture. Toss well and sprinkle cinnamon on top of salad.

CRANBERRY FLUFF

2 cups raw cranberries, ground
¾ cup sugar
3 cups mini marshmallows
1 cup diced apples
2 cups seedless grapes
1 (8 ounce) carton nondairy whipped topping

Combine cranberries, sugar, and marshmallows. Cover and chill overnight. Add apples and grapes; mix well. Fold in whipped topping and chill.

STAINED GLASS FRUIT SALAD

1 (15 ounce) can chunk pineapple
3 bananas, sliced
1 (11 ounce) can mandarin oranges, drained
1 (16 ounce) can peach pie filling
1 (10 ounce) package frozen strawberries, not in juice, partially thawed
1 cup blueberries

Drain pineapple, reserving juice. Cut bananas in slices and put in pineapple juice, stirring to coat all slices. Let bananas remain in juice; set aside. In large bowl, combine oranges, pie filling, strawberries, and pineapple. Drain juice from bananas and add to fruit mixture. Mix thoroughly and chill for at least one hour. Add blueberries just before serving.

ASPARAGUS SALAD

1½ pounds fresh asparagus
1 small red onion, cut into rings
2 teaspoons lemon pepper
1 tablespoon Dijon mustard

1 tablespoon red wine
   vinegar
½ teaspoon sugar
⅛ cup olive oil

Trim asparagus. Cook spears in a small amount of salted water, until crisp and tender. Do not overcook. Rinse with cold water. Drain. Place on platter or individual plates. Top with onion rings, if serving individual plates. Combine lemon pepper, Dijon, vinegar, sugar, and olive oil in a glass jar. Shake vigorously right before pouring over asparagus. May be served room temperature or chilled.

CHRISTMAS CRANBERRY SALAD

1 (6 ounce) package orange powdered gelatin mix
1 (16 ounce) can whole cranberry sauce
1 (16 ounce) can crushed pineapple, packed in own juice
1 (12 ounce) can ginger ale or cherry soda

Place gelatin mix and cranberry sauce in saucepan and bring to a boil. Stir in pineapple. Add soda. When bubbling stops, pour into 5-cup mold or bowl. If desired, chopped nuts may be added.

MIXED GREEN SALAD WITH RASPBERRIES AND RASPBERRY VINAIGRETTE

9 cups loosely packed mixed salad greens, washed and dried

1 teaspoon salt

1½ teaspoons Dijon-style mustard

3 tablespoons raspberry vinegar

4½ tablespoons vegetable oil

3 tablespoons olive oil

⅓ cup fresh raspberries, plus extra for garnish

⅓ cup walnuts

¼ cup Asiago cheese, shredded

Whole strawberries

Place the greens in a salad bowl and set in the refrigerator. Whisk together salt, mustard, vinegar, and oils. Mash raspberries and stir in. Toss dressing with greens and arrange on individual salad plates. Top each plate with walnuts, Asiago cheese, and a few whole strawberries.

LAYERED BLT SALAD

1 (8 ounce) carton sour cream
1 cup mayonnaise
1 tablespoon lemon juice
1 teaspoon basil
½ teaspoon salt
½ teaspoon pepper
¼ teaspoon garlic powder

1 large head iceberg or
   red leaf lettuce
1 (32 ounce) package thick
   bacon, cooked and crumbled
6 plum tomatoes
3 cups large croutons

Stir together sour cream, mayonnaise, lemon juice, basil, salt, pepper, and garlic powder. Layer lettuce, bacon, and tomato in 9x13-inch pan. Spread mayonnaise mixture evenly over tomatoes, sealing to edge of dish. Cover and chill 2 hours. Sprinkle with croutons.

ALL THE TRIMMINGS: SIDES

Sing hey! Sing hey!
For Christmas Day;
Twine mistletoe and holly.
For a friendship glows
In winter snows,
And so let's all be jolly!

UNKNOWN

CHRISTMAS CRANBERRY CASSEROLE

1 (16 ounce) package fresh cranberries
3 cups apples, diced
1½ teaspoons lemon juice
¾ cup sugar

Topping:
1⅓ cups oatmeal
1 cup walnuts, chopped
⅓ cup brown sugar
½ cup butter, melted

Preheat oven to 325 degrees. Blend cranberries, apples, lemon juice, and sugar together in a bowl. Pour into greased 8x8-inch baking dish. Combine oatmeal, walnuts, brown sugar, and butter. Evenly spread over cranberry mixture. Bake uncovered 45 to 60 minutes. If top starts to get too dark, cover with foil. Serve immediately.

SWEET POTATO CASSEROLE

3 cups sweet potatoes, mashed
1 cup sugar
½ teaspoon salt
2 eggs

¼ cup butter
½ cup milk
1 teaspoon vanilla

Preheat oven to 350 degrees. Combine above ingredients in greased 8x8-inch baking dish.

For topping, combine:
1 cup brown sugar
1 cup pecans, chopped
½ cup flour
¼ cup butter, melted

Sprinkle topping ingredients over potatoes. Bake 30 minutes.

CORN PUDDING

½ cup butter
1 (16 ounce) can whole kernel corn, drained
1 (16 ounce) can creamed corn
1 (8 ounce) carton sour cream
1 box cornbread mix

Preheat oven to 350 degrees. Melt butter in casserole. Add corn and sour cream. Mix well. Sprinkle cornbread mix over corn and stir together. Bake 45 minutes.

ALMOST DESSERT POTATOES

10 medium potatoes
½ cup butter, melted
1 (8 ounce) package cheddar cheese, shredded
2 tablespoons chives, chopped
3 tablespoons ranch dressing
2 cups sour cream
Salt and pepper to taste

Bake potatoes in foil at 400 degrees for 40 minutes or until slightly firm. Remove from foil and cool in refrigerator overnight. Peel potatoes and grate into large mixing bowl. Stir together remaining ingredients. Pour mixture into greased 2½-quart casserole and bake at 350 degrees for 30 to 40 minutes or until lightly browned.

BROCCOLI CHEESE CASSEROLE

½ cup onion, chopped
½ cup butter, melted, divided
1 (10½ ounce) can cream of mushroom soup
1 (4 ounce) can sliced mushrooms, drained
1 (6 ounce) roll garlic cheese, chopped
Salt and pepper to taste
¼ cup slivered almonds
3 cups frozen chopped broccoli
2 cups herb-seasoned stuffing mix

Preheat oven to 350 degrees. In a heavy skillet, sauté onion in ¼ cup butter until onion is tender. Combine cooked onion, soup, mushrooms, garlic cheese, salt, pepper, almonds, and broccoli; mix well. Spoon broccoli cheese casserole mixture into a lightly buttered 2-quart casserole. Combine stuffing mix and ¼ cup melted butter; spoon over broccoli casserole. Bake 30 minutes.

GLAZED CARROTS WITH GINGER AND HONEY

Salt
2 pounds baby carrots
2 tablespoons unsalted butter
2 (2-inch) pieces fresh ginger, peeled and julienned
3 tablespoons honey

Bring a medium pot of water to a boil. Salt water, add carrots, and reduce heat. Simmer until carrots are almost tender, 3 to 4 minutes. Remove carrots from heat; drain. (Carrots can be prepared earlier in the day.) Melt butter in a large skillet over medium-high heat. Add ginger and sauté, stirring until transparent (about 2 minutes). Add carrots and honey and cook for 4 to 5 minutes, or until carrots are glazed. Serve immediately.

"SWEET" POTATO GRATIN

2 pounds yellow potatoes
1 cup ricotta cheese, divided
Salt and pepper to taste
Nutmeg to taste
1 egg
1 cup heavy cream

1 cup Gruyere cheese,
shredded, divided
¼ cup Parmesan cheese,
shredded, divided
Sweet butter

Peel potatoes and slice very thinly. Drop into a pot of cold, salted water. Boil for 1 minute; drain and rinse with cold water. Drain again and pat dry. Season ricotta with salt, pepper, and nutmeg to taste. Slightly beat egg and add enough heavy cream to make 1 cup liquid. Season with salt, pepper, and nutmeg. Mix the shredded cheeses together. Lightly grease a shallow 9x12-inch baking dish with butter. Arrange a layer of slightly overlapping potato slices in the dish. Dot with about ⅓ of ricotta mixture. Sprinkle with ⅓ of the shredded cheeses. Repeat, using all of the ingredients and ending with a potato layer. Gently pour the egg and cream mixture into the dish, lifting potato slices with a fork if necessary to allow the cream to spread evenly. Bake on the center rack of a preheated 350-degree oven for 35 to 45 minutes, or until potatoes are tender and cheese is browned and bubbling. Let stand about 10 minutes before serving.

HOLIDAY STUFFING

2 loaves Italian bread (about 10 ounces each), torn into bite-size pieces
4 tablespoons butter, room temperature, plus more for baking dish
4 celery stalks, thinly sliced
4 shallots, minced
2 garlic cloves, minced
Coarse salt and ground pepper
½ cup white grape juice
½ cup parsley leaves, chopped
3 large eggs, lightly beaten
1½ teaspoons salt
¼ teaspoon pepper
2 (14½ ounce) cans reduced-sodium chicken broth

Preheat oven to 400 degrees. Arrange bread in a single layer on two rimmed baking sheets. Bake until crisp but not browned, about 10 minutes, rotating sheets halfway through. In a large saucepan, melt butter over medium heat. Add celery, shallots, and garlic; season with salt and pepper. Cook, stirring occasionally, until vegetables are softened (5 to 7 minutes). Add grape juice and cook until evaporated (3 to 5 minutes). Transfer to a large bowl.

To vegetables in bowl, add bread, parsley, and eggs. Season with 1½ teaspoons salt and ¼ teaspoon pepper; stir to combine. Mix in half of broth. Continue to add in more broth just until stuffing is moistened but not wet (there should not be any liquid in the bottom of the bowl).

Just before roasting turkey, stuff it with 4 cups stuffing. Spoon remaining stuffing into a buttered 8x8-inch baking dish. Cover with buttered aluminum foil and refrigerate. When turkey is removed from oven to rest, place covered baking dish in oven, and bake until warmed through, 25 to 30 minutes. Uncover and bake until golden, about 15 minutes more.

CREAMED CROCK-POT CORN

1 (16 ounce) package frozen corn
1 (8 ounce) package cream cheese
2 tablespoons butter
Sugar, salt, pepper, and garlic powder to taste

Combine all ingredients and cook on low for approximately 2 hours.

BROCCOLI WITH CASHEWS

1 large bunch fresh broccoli or
   2 (10 ounce) packages frozen broccoli
2 tablespoons onion, minced
2 tablespoons butter
1 cup sour cream
2 teaspoons sugar

1 teaspoon vinegar
½ teaspoon poppy seeds
¼ teaspoon salt
½ teaspoon paprika
1 cup roasted cashews

Preheat oven to 325 degrees. Cook broccoli in water until crisp. Sauté onion in butter. Stir in sour cream and remaining ingredients, except cashews. Layer broccoli in a buttered 1½-quart baking dish and cover with sauce. Sprinkle with cashews and bake uncovered 25 minutes.

GIFT-WRAPPED GREEN BEANS

1 pound fresh green beans
½ teaspoon salt
3 strips bacon, cut in half
½ to 1 cup French dressing

String beans. Trim tips so beans are uniform in length. Bring 2 inches of water to boil in large saucepan. Add beans and salt. Simmer uncovered 5 minutes. Cover and continue to simmer 10 to 12 minutes or until tender-crisp. Remove from heat and plunge in cold water to stop cooking; drain.

Divide green beans into 6 bunches. Wrap each bunch with bacon and secure with toothpick. Place in a 9x9-inch baking dish. Pour dressing over beans and marinate a minimum of 1 hour in refrigerator. Bake with marinade 30 minutes in preheated 350-degree oven.

YULETIDE BOUNTY: BREADS

'Twas the night before Christmas, when all through the house
Not a creature was stirring, not even a mouse;
The stockings were hung by the chimney with care,
In hopes that St. Nicholas soon would be there.

CLEMENT C. MOORE

CHOCOLATE CHIP PUMPKIN MUFFINS

¾ cup sugar
¼ cup vegetable oil
2 eggs
¾ cup canned pumpkin
¼ cup water
1½ cups flour
¾ teaspoon baking powder
½ teaspoon baking soda
¼ teaspoon ground cloves

½ teaspoon cinnamon
¼ teaspoon nutmeg
¼ teaspoon salt
½ cup semisweet
     chocolate chips

Preheat oven to 400 degrees. Grease and flour muffin pan or use paper liners. Mix sugar, oil, and eggs. Add pumpkin and water. In separate bowl, mix together the flour, baking powder, baking soda, spices, and salt. Add pumpkin mixture and stir in chocolate chips. Fill muffin cups ⅔ full with batter. Bake 20 to 25 minutes.

STRAWBERRY BREAD

1 (10 ounce) package frozen strawberries, undrained
2 eggs
½ cup plus 2 tablespoons vegetable oil
1½ cups flour
½ teaspoon baking soda
½ teaspoon salt
1½ teaspoons cinnamon
1 cup sugar
¾ cup pecans, chopped

In a large mixing bowl, mix strawberries, eggs, and oil. In a separate bowl, mix dry ingredients and nuts. Stir dry ingredients into strawberry mixture, mixing well. Bake in greased 9x5-inch loaf pan for about 60 minutes or until toothpick comes out clean.

PARMESAN CRESCENT ROLLS

¾ cup butter, room temperature
1 (16 ounce) package small-curd cottage cheese
⅛ teaspoon salt
2 cups flour
1 cup grated Parmesan cheese, divided

Blend butter, cottage cheese, and salt in a large bowl. Gently mix in flour. Dough will be sticky. Divide dough into 4 equal balls. Cover and refrigerate until chilled, at least 1 hour. Preheat oven to 400 degrees. Flour a surface lightly and roll 1 ball of dough into a flat circle using a rolling pin. Sprinkle the circle with ¼ cup Parmesan cheese. Using a knife or pizza cutter, cut the circle into 8 equal pieces. Take 1 slice of dough and roll into crescent shape, starting with the wide end and finishing with the triangle tip tucked under the roll. Place on greased baking sheet. Repeat with remaining slices and dough balls. Bake until golden brown, 20 to 25 minutes. Cool on pans for 10 minutes before removing to cool completely on a wire rack.

BANANA SOUR CREAM BREAD

¼ cup sugar
1 teaspoon cinnamon
¾ cup butter, softened
3 cups sugar
3 eggs
6 very ripe bananas, mashed
1 (16 ounce) container sour cream
2 teaspoons vanilla

2 teaspoons cinnamon
½ teaspoon salt
3 teaspoons baking soda
4½ cups flour
1 cup walnuts,
    chopped (optional)

Preheat oven to 300 degrees. Grease four 7x3-inch loaf pans. In small bowl, stir together ¼ cup sugar and 1 teaspoon cinnamon. Dust pans lightly with cinnamon sugar mixture. In large bowl, cream butter and 3 cups sugar. Mix in eggs, mashed bananas, sour cream, vanilla, and cinnamon. Mix in salt, baking soda, and flour. Stir in nuts. Divide into prepared pans. Bake 1 hour, until a toothpick inserted in center comes out clean.

LOW-FAT CRANBERRY BREAD

1½ cups wheat bran flakes
2 cups flour
1½ teaspoons baking powder
½ teaspoon baking soda
½ teaspoon salt

1 cup sugar
1 egg
2 tablespoons plain yogurt
1 cup orange juice
1 cup halved cranberries

Preheat oven to 325 degrees. In large mixing bowl, combine bran flakes and all other dry ingredients together. In small mixing bowl, beat egg until foamy; add remaining ingredients, mixing well. Add to dry mixture. Stir until mixed well. Bake in a greased loaf pan for 70 minutes. Yield: 1 loaf

APPLESAUCE BREAD

4 eggs
1½ cups sugar
1 cup oil
2 cups applesauce
⅔ cup milk
3½ cups flour

2 teaspoons baking soda
1 teaspoon cinnamon
1 teaspoon nutmeg
1 cup nuts, chopped
   (optional)

Preheat oven to 350 degrees. Beat together eggs, sugar, oil, applesauce, and milk. Sift together the flour, soda, cinnamon, and nutmeg; add to first mixture and mix well. Fold in nuts. Pour into three 8x4-inch pans and bake 1 hour.

PUMPKIN SWIRL BREAD

Filling:
1 (8 ounce) package cream cheese, softened
¼ cup sugar
1 egg, beaten

Batter:
1 cup canned pumpkin
½ cup butter, melted
1 egg, beaten
1¾ cups flour
1½ cups sugar
1 teaspoon baking soda
1 teaspoon cinnamon
½ teaspoon salt
¼ teaspoon nutmeg
⅓ cup water

Grease and flour 9x5-inch loaf pan. Combine cream cheese, sugar, and egg, mixing well until blended. In separate bowl, combine pumpkin, butter, and egg. In another bowl, combine dry ingredients. Add water and pumpkin mixture to dry ingredients, mixing just until moistened. Reserve 2 cups of batter. Pour remaining batter into loaf pan. Pour filling over batter; top with the 2 cups of pumpkin batter. Cut through batter with knife several times for swirl effect. Bake 1 hour and 10 minutes or until wooden pick inserted in center comes out clean. Cool 5 minutes and remove from pan.

DUTCH APPLE BREAD

1 cup sugar
½ cup butter, softened
2 eggs, unbeaten
2 tablespoons sour milk
2 cups flour
1 teaspoon baking soda
1 teaspoon salt
1 teaspoon vanilla
2 cups apples, finely chopped

Topping:
2 tablespoons sugar
2 tablespoons butter
Chopped nuts
2 tablespoons flour
1 teaspoon cinnamon

Preheat oven to 350 degrees. Cream sugar and butter. Blend in eggs and sour milk. In separate bowl, sift together flour, soda, and salt. Add to creamed mixture. Mix in vanilla and apples. Pour into greased 9x5-inch loaf pan. Combine topping ingredients; cut through until crumbly. Sprinkle over batter in pan. Bake 1 hour. Cool 10 minutes and remove from pan.

BUTTER PECAN BREAD

2¼ cups sifted flour
2 teaspoons baking powder
½ teaspoon baking soda
½ teaspoon salt
½ teaspoon cinnamon
¼ teaspoon nutmeg
1 cup light brown sugar, packed

1 egg, beaten
1 cup buttermilk
2 tablespoons butter,
  melted
1 cup pecans,
  chopped

Preheat oven to 350 degrees. Sift together the flour, baking powder, soda, salt, and spices; blend in brown sugar. In separate bowl, combine egg, buttermilk, and butter; add to flour mixture, stirring to blend well. Stir in chopped nuts. Turn batter into a greased and floured 9x5-inch loaf pan. Bake 45 to 50 minutes or until a toothpick inserted in center comes out clean and is just slightly tacky.

HONEY & WHEAT ROLLS

2 teaspoons dry yeast
1 cup warm water
1 teaspoon salt
¼ cup honey
1 egg, beaten
2 cups bread flour
1¼ cups whole wheat flour

Dissolve yeast in warm water. Add salt, honey, and egg; mix well. Stir in as much flour as possible, then knead in the rest. Knead thoroughly for 6 to 9 minutes. Place dough in greased bowl and cover with a cloth. Let rise until double in size (1 to 2 hours). Form into rolls as desired. Bake at 350 degrees for 20 to 25 minutes.

NO-KNEAD DINNER ROLLS

½ cup sugar
1 teaspoon salt
¼ cup butter, softened
¾ cup boiling water
¾ cup cold water

1 egg, beaten
1 package dry yeast
½ cup warm water
5½ cups flour

In a large mixing bowl, combine sugar, salt, and butter. Pour ¾ cup boiling water over mixture, stirring well. Add ¾ cup cold water. Add beaten egg. Dissolve yeast in ½ cup warm water and add to egg mixture. Stir in flour. To bake, place in a greased bowl, grease side up, and let rise in a warm place 2½ hours. Shape rolls and bake at 325 degrees for 25 minutes. Dough will keep for about 10 days in refrigerator.

POPPY SEED BREAD

2 cups flour
1 teaspoon salt
1 teaspoon baking powder
2 eggs
¾ cup oil
1½ cups sugar

1 cup skim milk
1 tablespoon poppy seeds
1 teaspoon vanilla
1 teaspoon almond extract
1 teaspoon butter flavoring

Glaze:
¼ cup orange juice
½ cup sugar
½ teaspoon vanilla

½ teaspoon almond extract
½ teaspoon butter flavoring

Preheat oven to 350 degrees. Combine all bread ingredients. Beat 2 minutes. Pour into greased 9x5-inch loaf pan. Bake 1 hour and 15 minutes or until done. Combine glaze ingredients and pour over warm loaf.

1½ cups flour
4 tablespoons butter or margarine
½ teaspoon baking soda
1 teaspoon cream of tartar
1 teaspoon salt
1 tablespoon sugar
⅔ cup milk
½ cup raisins

Preheat oven to 400 degrees. Cut butter into flour until it resembles bread crumbs. Stir in other dry ingredients. Mix milk in, stirring with a fork. Add raisins. Roll out dough to 1 inch thick. Cut in circles. Place on greased cookie sheet; brush with milk and bake for 10 minutes at 400 degrees.

ONE-RISE CINNAMON ROLLS

1 cup heavy whipping cream
1 cup brown sugar
3 to 3 ½ cups flour
¼ cup sugar
1 cup hot water
1 egg
1 package dry yeast
1 teaspoon salt
2 tablespoons butter, softened
½ cup sugar
½ cup butter, softened
2 teaspoons cinnamon
Chopped nuts (optional)

Mix cream and brown sugar in ungreased 9x13-inch pan. In large bowl, blend 1½ cups flour with ¼ cup sugar, water, egg, yeast, salt, and 2 tablespoons butter. Beat on medium speed for 3 minutes and stir in remaining flour. Knead on floured surface for 1 minute. Roll dough into 15x7-inch rectangle.

Mix ½ cup sugar, ½ cup softened butter, 2 tablespoons cinnamon, and chopped nuts (if desired) to make filling. Spread filling over dough, starting at long side. Roll tightly and seal edges. Cut into 20 rolls and place cut side down on cream mixture. Cover and let rise until doubled (35 to 40 minutes). Bake at 400 degrees for 25 minutes. Cool 10 to 15 minutes before turning out onto serving tray.

FAVORITE CRESCENT ROLLS

2 tablespoons sugar
6 tablespoons shortening, softened
1 teaspoon salt
2 packages dry yeast
1½ cups lukewarm milk
4 cups flour, sifted
Butter
Celery or sesame seed

Mix together sugar, shortening, and salt until smooth. Add yeast to milk and stir until dissolved. Beat in flour. Scrape dough from sides of bowl as you mix. Let rise in warm place until doubled, about 30 minutes. Shape into crescents or butterhorns. Brush with butter and celery or sesame seed. Bake 12 minutes in 425-degree oven.

HEARTY HOLIDAY GOODNESS: MAIN DISHES

O Christmas Sun! What holy task is thine!
To fold a world in the embrace of God!

GUY WETMORE CARRYL

HAM CRANBERRY RAISIN SANDWICHES

1 (8 ounce) package cream cheese, softened
½ cup whole berry cranberry sauce
28 slices cinnamon raisin bread, crusts removed
1½ pounds deli ham, thinly sliced

Combine cream cheese and cranberry sauce, stirring well. Spread mixture on each bread slice. Top with ham. Place a second slice of bread on top with cream cheese mixture also spread on it to form a sandwich. Cut each sandwich into four triangles.

MANICOTTI CREPES

1 cup small curd cottage cheese
3 ounces cream cheese, softened
2 tablespoons butter, softened
2 tablespoons parsley, chopped
1 egg, beaten
1 tablespoon green onion,
    chopped

⅛ teaspoon salt
8 cooked crepes
    (see recipe on p. 112)
1 (15 ounce) can marinara
    sauce
¼ cup Parmesan cheese,
    grated

In a medium mixing bowl, combine cottage cheese, cream cheese, butter, parsley, egg, green onion, and salt. Spoon 3 tablespoons of cheese mixture into center of each cooked crepe. Roll up. Place in a shallow baking dish. Pour marinara sauce over filled crepes. Sprinkle with Parmesan cheese. Bake at 350 degrees for 20 to 30 minutes.

CREPES

2 eggs, beaten
1½ cups milk
1 cup flour
1 tablespoon cooking oil
¼ teaspoon salt

Combine all ingredients in a mixing bowl; beat well. To cook, heat a lightly greased 6-inch skillet; remove from heat. Add 2 tablespoons batter to hot skillet; lift and tilt to spread batter. Return to heat and brown on one side only. Invert onto paper towel and remove crepe. Repeat with remaining batter, greasing skillet occasionally.

RIGATONI WITH ASPARAGUS AND GORGONZOLA SAUCE

1½ pounds asparagus, trimmed and cut into ½-inch pieces
2 cups Gorgonzola cheese
3¼ cups heavy cream
1 pound rigatoni
Fresh ground black pepper
Grated Parmesan cheese

Cook asparagus in boiling, salted water until tender, about 4 minutes. Drain and set aside. Place Gorgonzola and cream in a saucepan. Cook over medium-low heat until mixture is smooth. Cook pasta al dente. Drain well. Add sauce to pasta. Toss to coat. Stir in asparagus and season to taste. Serve with freshly grated Parmesan cheese.

CINNAMON-APRICOT GLAZED SALMON

2 tablespoons low-sodium soy sauce
1 tablespoon fresh ginger, peeled and minced
2 (3-inch) cinnamon sticks
1 (12 ounce) can apricot nectar
4 (6 ounce) salmon fillets, about 1 inch thick

In a saucepan combine soy sauce, ginger, cinnamon sticks, and nectar. Bring to a boil. Reduce heat. Simmer mixture until reduced to ¾ cup, about 30 minutes. Strain the apricot mixture through a sieve over a bowl. Discard solids. Preheat broiler or grill. Broil or grill 5 minutes. Brush fish with ¼ cup mixture. Broil or grill until lightly browned and fish flakes easily. To serve, pour remaining glaze over fish.

FAVORITE FLANK STEAK

1 flank steak
Lemon pepper to taste
¼ to ½ cup Worcestershire sauce

Place flank steak in baking dish lined with foil. Sprinkle lemon pepper to taste on steak, along with ¼ to ½ cup Worcestershire sauce. Broil in oven 10 to 15 minutes on middle rack. Turn the steak over. Add more lemon pepper and sauce. Let broil 10 to 15 minutes longer. Check middle for doneness. Should be medium-rare. Cook longer for desired doneness.

CHICKEN PISTACHIO ROLL-UPS
WITH FRUIT SAUCE

6 whole boneless,
   skinless chicken breasts (halved)
¾ teaspoon salt
¼ teaspoon pepper
3 tablespoons butter

1 (8 ounce) carton fresh
   mushrooms, chopped
½ cup pistachio nuts,
   chopped
¾ cup soft bread crumbs

With rolling pin, flatten chicken between waxed paper to an even thickness. Sprinkle with salt and pepper. In small skillet, melt butter. Sauté mushrooms and ½ cup chopped pistachios over medium heat, until all liquid evaporates. Stir in bread crumbs. Cool. Divide mixture into 12 equal portions. Spoon 1 portion onto center of each breast half. Roll jellyroll fashion. Arrange, seam side down, in 9x13-inch glass baking dish. Prepare fruit sauce (see p. 117); divide and spoon half of sauce over rolls. (Reserve remaining sauce in refrigerator until serving time.) Refrigerate, covered, up to 24 hours. Heat oven to 350 degrees. Bake uncovered until chicken is tender and juices run clear (about 40 minutes), basting once or twice. To serve, arrange on heated serving platter. Heat remaining sauce and spoon over chicken. Garnish with remaining pistachios. Makes 12 servings.

Fruit sauce:
4 teaspoons cornstarch
½ cup apple cider vinegar
1 tablespoon sugar
½ cup water

½ cup butter, melted
½ cup apricot preserves
½ cup colonial chutney

In small saucepan, combine cornstarch, vinegar, sugar, and water until smooth. Stir in melted butter, apricot preserves, and colonial chutney. Cook over medium heat, stirring constantly, until thickened.

STICKY CHICKEN

6 to 10 chicken breast halves, cut in halves or thirds
Small slices of Swiss or havarti cheese (enough to cover each chicken
  portion)
2 (16 ounce) cans cream of chicken soup
½ cup white grape juice
½ cup butter, melted
1 box stuffing mix

Preheat oven to 350 degrees. Spray a 9x13-inch pan with cooking spray. Place chicken pieces in pan. Top each with a slice of cheese. Combine soup and grape juice; pour over chicken. Combine butter and stuffing; spread on top of all. Bake 1 hour, uncovered.

BARBECUED MEATBALLS

1 egg, lightly beaten
1 can evaporated milk
1 cup quick-cooking oats
½ cup onion, finely chopped
1 teaspoon salt
1 teaspoon chili powder
¼ teaspoon garlic powder
¼ teaspoon pepper
    (optional)

1½ pounds ground beef

Sauce:

1 cup ketchup
¾ cup packed brown sugar
¼ cup onion, chopped
½ teaspoon liquid smoke

Preheat oven to 350 degrees. In a bowl, combine the first eight ingredients. Crumble beef over mixture and mix well. Shape into 1-inch balls and place in greased 9x13-inch baking dish. Bake uncovered 18 to 20 minutes, or until meat is no longer pink. Combine sauce ingredients in a saucepan. Bring to boil. Reduce heat and simmer 2 minutes, stirring frequently. Pour over meatballs. Bake 10 minutes longer.

BARBECUED WHOLE PORK TENDERLOIN

3 large pork tenderloins

Marinade:
1 cup soy sauce
⅓ cup sesame oil
3 large cloves garlic, minced
1 tablespoon ginger

Sauce:
1 (19 ounce) bottle barbecue
   sauce
⅓ cup soy sauce
¼ cup sesame oil
1 large clove garlic, minced

In a small bowl, mix together marinade ingredients. Pour marinade over meat in glass or enameled pan. Cover and marinate in refrigerator at least 5 to 6 hours. Place tenderloins over a low fire on charcoal grill. Barbecue with lid closed, turning every 15 minutes and basting with sauce mixture, approximately 1½ hours or until done. (For indoor barbecuing, use a 300-degree preheated oven. Follow basting directions and cook to desired doneness.)

CHICKEN DIVAN

1 package boneless chicken
1 (16 ounce) package frozen broccoli
1 can cream of chicken soup
1 tablespoon mayonnaise
¼ cup milk
Colby and monterey jack cheese, cubed

Bake chicken in oven at 350 degrees. Turn once. Bake until cooked (about 20 minutes). Cut up in small cubes. In large casserole, combine chicken and broccoli. In small bowl, combine soup, mayonnaise, and milk. Pour over broccoli/chicken mixture. Put cubed cheeses on top of mixture. Bake at 350 degrees 30 to 45 minutes.

HAM BALLS

Meat mixture:
1 (16 ounce) smoked ham
1½ pounds pork shoulder
2 cups bread crumbs
1½ cups milk
2 eggs, beaten
Salt and pepper

Sauce:
¾ cup brown sugar
½ cup water
½ cup vinegar
1 teaspoon dry mustard

Preheat oven to 325 degrees. Grind ham and pork shoulder together. Combine all meat mixture ingredients together and form into balls. Arrange in shallow baking pan. Combine all sauce ingredients and mix well with wire whisk. Pour over balls. Bake 1 hour. Baste balls with sauce a few times while baking.

CHICKEN CRESCENT ALMONDINE

3 cups cooked, diced chicken
1 (15 ounce) can cream of
   chicken soup
1 (8 ounce) can sliced
   water chestnuts, drained
4 ounces mushrooms, sliced
½ cup onions, chopped

½ cup celery, chopped
½ cup sour cream
½ cup mayonnaise
1 tube crescent roll dough
⅔ cup Swiss cheese, grated
½ cup slivered almonds
4 tablespoons butter, melted

Preheat oven to 350 degrees. Combine first 8 ingredients in a pan on the stove; heat until thick and bubbly. Spread into a greased 9x13-inch pan. Top with rectangle of crescent roll dough. Mix Swiss cheese, almonds, and butter; sprinkle on top of dough. Bake 25 minutes.

HOAGIE CREPES

Crepes:

2 eggs, beaten
1½ cups milk
1 cup flour

1 tablespoon oil
¼ teaspoon salt

Combine all ingredients in a mixing bowl; beat well. To cook, heat a lightly greased 6-inch skillet; remove from heat. Add 2 tablespoons batter to hot skillet; lift and tilt to spread batter. Return to heat and brown on one side only. Invert onto paper towel and remove crepe. Repeat with remaining batter, greasing skillet occasionally.

Crepe filling:

Thin sliced ham
Hard salami
Provolone cheese

Shredded lettuce
Chopped tomato
Grilled onions

Dressing:
4 tablespoons olive oil
2 tablespoons plus 1 teaspoon red wine vinegar
1 teaspoon salt
¼ teaspoon oregano
¼ teaspoon dry mustard
1 clove garlic, crushed

Place one slice of each meat and cheese in crepe. Top with lettuce, tomato, and onion. Combine dressing ingredients; pour approximately ½ teaspoon dressing over ingredients in crepe. Fold crepe over; top with one slice cheese. Bake at 350 degrees 15 to 20 minutes. Can be frozen and reheated.

PORK TENDERLOIN WITH CREAMY MUSTARD SAUCE

1 pound pork tenderloin
Salt and pepper to taste
1 teaspoon vegetable oil

½ cup evaporated milk
2 tablespoons Dijon mustard
2 green onions, sliced

Cut pork into 1-inch-thick slices. Place pork between two pieces of plastic wrap. Flatten to ¼-inch thickness using meat mallet or rolling pin. Season with salt and ground black pepper. Heat oil in large skillet over medium-high heat. Add half of pork; cook each side for 2 minutes or until browned and cooked through. Remove from skillet; set aside and keep warm. Repeat with remaining pork. Reduce heat to low. Add evaporated milk; stir to loosen brown bits from bottom of skillet. Stir in mustard and green onions. Return pork to skillet. Cook for 1 to 2 minutes or until sauce is lightly thickened, turning pork to coat with sauce.

APRICOT-GLAZED HAM

1 (5 pound) fully cooked whole boneless ham
⅓ cup brown sugar, firmly packed
1 tablespoon cornstarch
½ teaspoon nutmeg
¼ teaspoon ground cloves
⅔ cup apricot nectar
2 tablespoons lemon juice

Place ham on rack in shallow roasting pan. Bake uncovered in a 325-degree oven for 1 to 1½ hours or until meat thermometer registers 140 degrees. For the glaze, combine brown sugar, cornstarch, nutmeg, and cloves in a small saucepan. Stir in apricot nectar and lemon juice. Cook over medium heat until thickened and bubbly, stirring constantly. Brush ham with glaze. Continue baking 15 to 20 minutes more, brushing occasionally with glaze.

FETTUCCINE WITH LEMON GARLIC SHRIMP

1 (9 ounce) package fettuccine
3 tablespoons butter or margarine
¼ cup onion, chopped
4 cloves garlic, chopped
1 (14½ ounce) can chicken broth
2 tablespoons cornstarch
1 pound medium shrimp, peeled and deveined
¼ cup fresh flat-leaf parsley, chopped
3 tablespoons fresh lemon juice
2 tablespoons Parmesan cheese, freshly grated

Prepare pasta according to package directions. Melt butter in large skillet. Add onion and garlic; cook until onion is tender. Add chicken broth and cornstarch; mix until smooth. Cook until sauce is thickened and translucent. Add shrimp, parsley, and lemon juice; cook until shrimp turns pink. Toss pasta with shrimp mixture. Garnish with Parmesan cheese.

BROILED CITRUS SALMON

2 tablespoons olive oil
1 tablespoon lime juice
1 tablespoon lemon juice
2 teaspoons molasses
⅛ teaspoon salt

⅛ teaspoon pepper
4 (5 ounce) salmon fillets
  or steaks
Juice of 1 orange

Preheat broiler. In small bowl, stir together olive oil, lime juice, lemon juice, molasses, salt, and pepper; mix well. Place salmon on broiling pan, skin-side down. Brush liberally with marinade and broil until crisp on the outside and flesh flakes easily, about 7 minutes per inch of thickness. Remove from broiler and sprinkle immediately with orange juice. Serve hot.

1 gallon water
1 cup salt
½ cup lime juice
½ cup apple juice
3 to 4 limes, halved
2 lemons, halved
1 orange, halved
1 (18 to 22 pound) turkey
1 turkey brining bag or container big enough to hold turkey
½ cup butter, softened
Salt and pepper to taste

Warm water over stove and dissolve the salt. Let cool completely. Add lime juice and apple juice. Squeeze citrus into the liquid and add the rinds to it. Rinse the turkey and place in brining bag or other container. The turkey must be completely covered in liquid. Cover with the brining solution and marinate overnight or up to 24 hours. Remove turkey, rinse, and pat dry. Rub turkey all over with the butter, sprinkle with salt and pepper, and drape with cheesecloth. Place turkey breast side up on roasting pan rack. Four to five hours before serving is scheduled, place turkey in a preheated 325-degree oven. Baste every 30 to 40 minutes with melted butter at first, then with its own juices. Roast 3½ to 4½ hours until juices run clear. When turkey is done, remove and cover with foil to rest 30 minutes before carving.

SWEET TREATS: DESSERTS

Blessed is the season which engages the
whole world in a conspiracy of love!

HAMILTON WRIGHT MABIE

CHOCOLATE CHEESECAKE

Crust:
1½ cups crushed chocolate wafer cookies
½ cup almonds, finely chopped
¼ cup butter, melted

Filling:
2 (8 ounce) packages cream cheese
⅔ cup sugar
3 eggs
1 (12 ounce) package chocolate chips, melted and cooled
1 cup whipping cream, not beaten
2 tablespoons butter, melted
1 teaspoon vanilla

Topping:
1 cup sour cream
1½ teaspoons vanilla
1 teaspoon sugar

Preheat oven to 325 degrees. Grease 9-inch springform pan. Mix crust ingredients well and press on bottom and sides of pan. Beat filling ingredients until smooth, adding one egg at a time. Bake 55 to 65 minutes in shallow pan with ½ inch water. Place on lower rack to prevent cracking.

NEW YEAR'S EVE
SMORGASBORD RICE PUDDING

6 cups whole milk
½ to ⅔ cup instant rice
½ teaspoon salt
½ cup raisins
6 eggs, slightly beaten

¾ cup sugar
2 teaspoons vanilla
Cinnamon
Nutmeg

Preheat oven to 375 degrees. Mix milk, rice, salt, and raisins in a 3-quart pan; bring to boil. Reduce heat and simmer for 10 minutes. Mix eggs and sugar in 3-quart bowl. Slowly add milk mixture to eggs and sugar; add vanilla. Place in a greased 2-quart casserole. Carefully place casserole dish in pan of water in oven. Do not cover. Bake 45 minutes to 1 hour. Stir 3 times, approximately 10 minutes apart. Sprinkle with cinnamon or nutmeg after third stir.

GINGERBREAD CAKE

Vegetable oil
1 (15 ounce) can pumpkin
⅓ cup molasses
3 eggs
2 tablespoons pumpkin pie spice
1 package German chocolate cake mix

Preheat oven to 350 degrees. Brush 9x13-inch pan with vegetable oil. Whisk pumpkin, molasses, eggs, and spice until smooth. Add cake mix until thoroughly blended. Pour batter into pan, spreading evenly. Bake 40 to 45 minutes until toothpick comes out clean. Sprinkle with powdered sugar or serve with whipping cream.

VELVET CUTOUTS

1 cup butter
3 ounces cream cheese
1 cup sugar
1 egg
1 teaspoon vanilla
2½ cups flour

Preheat oven to 350 degrees. Cream together butter, cream cheese, and sugar. Add egg and vanilla and beat well. Stir in flour. Chill 1 to 2 hours. Roll about ¼ inch thick, then cut into shapes. Place on baking sheet; bake 10 to 12 minutes.

JELLY BELLIES

½ cup butter, softened
¼ cup brown sugar
1 egg, separated
1 teaspoon vanilla
1 cup sifted flour
½ cup nuts, finely chopped

Jam of choice
4 tablespoons powdered sugar
2 teaspoons milk

Preheat oven to 375 degrees. Mix butter, sugar, egg yolk, and vanilla until smooth. Stir in flour. Roll into balls, then into slightly beaten egg white, then nuts. Press into center with thumb. Bake 8 minutes, then press into center again. Spoon one teaspoonful of jam onto center of cookie. Glaze with combined powdered sugar and milk.

TOASTED COCONUT PIE

1 scant cup sugar
½ cup flour
¼ teaspoon salt
2 cups milk, scalded
3 egg yolks

2 tablespoons butter
¾ teaspoon vanilla
1 cup flaked coconut
1 baked pastry shell
Meringue

In large saucepan, combine sugar, flour, and salt; slowly add milk. Add beaten egg yolks. Cook over medium heat, stirring vigorously until mixture thickens. Remove from heat, stir in firm butter, vanilla, and coconut. Pour into shell. Top with meringue; sprinkle with coconut and brown in hot oven for 1 minute, being careful not to overbake.

PUMPKIN CAKE

4 eggs
2 cups sugar
1 cup oil
2 cups canned pumpkin

2 cups flour
2 teaspoons baking soda
2 teaspoons cinnamon

Preheat oven to 350 degrees. Blend together eggs, sugar, oil, and pumpkin. Mix in dry ingredients. Pour into greased and floured 9x13-inch baking pan. Bake 25 to 30 minutes.

Frosting:
½ cup butter, softened
1 (8 ounce) package cream cheese

2 teaspoons vanilla
2 cups powdered sugar

Blend all frosting ingredients together with mixer. Spread over cooled cake. Top with chopped walnuts if desired.

CHOCOLATE-COVERED COCONUT BALLS

½ cup butter, melted
2 cups pecans, chopped
2 pounds powdered sugar
1 (15 ounce) can sweetened condensed milk
1 pound coconut
Candy making chocolate bar

Pour butter over pecans. Mix together next 3 ingredients. Combine both groups well. Form into 1-inch balls. Melt dipping chocolate. Dip coconut balls in chocolate; set on waxed paper to cool and harden.

GRANDMA'S SPRITZ

1 cup butter, softened
⅔ cup sugar
1 egg, beaten
½ teaspoon almond extract
½ teaspoon vanilla
2¼ cups flour (or more)
1 teaspoon baking powder

Preheat oven to 400 degrees. Cream butter and sugar. Add egg, almond extract, and vanilla. In separate bowl, sift flour and baking powder and add slowly to butter mixture. Chill in refrigerator. Press dough through a cookie press onto ungreased cookie sheets. Bake 7 to 10 minutes, being careful not to brown.

HOLIDAY MINI OATMEAL COOKIES

1 cup butter, softened
¾ cup sugar
½ teaspoon vanilla
2 cups quick-cooking oats
1 cup flour
1 teaspoon baking soda

Cream butter and sugar. Add vanilla and oatmeal. Gradually stir in flour and baking soda. Chill until semi-firm. Preheat oven to 325 degrees. Roll dough into little balls; press down with a fork. Sprinkle with red or green sugar. Bake 15 minutes. Makes 8 dozen.

MOLASSES SUGAR COOKIES

¾ cup butter
1 cup sugar
¼ cup molasses
1 egg
2 teaspoons baking soda
2 cups sifted flour

¼ teaspoon cloves
½ teaspoon ginger
1 teaspoon cinnamon
½ teaspoon salt
Granulated sugar
Powdered sugar for dusting

Melt butter; cool. Add sugar, molasses, and egg; beat well. In small bowl, combine dry ingredients, except granulated and powdered sugars. Mix well and chill.

Preheat oven to 375 degrees. Roll dough into 1-inch balls; roll in granulated sugar and place on ungreased cookie sheet about 2 inches apart. Bake 8 to 10 minutes. Cool on newspaper and sprinkle with powdered sugar. Makes 12 dozen.

SWEDISH ALMOND TOAST

4 cups flour
½ teaspoon baking powder
½ teaspoon baking soda
½ teaspoon salt
1 cup butter, softened

2 cups sugar
2 eggs
1 cup sour cream
1 teaspoon almond extract
Milk or cream

Preheat oven to 325 degrees. In small bowl, sift together dry ingredients. Set aside. In large bowl, cream butter and sugar. Beat in eggs, sour cream, and almond extract. Add dry mixture and blend. Spray 3 loaf pans with cooking spray. Divide batter and press down evenly in pans. Brush tops with milk or cream. Bake until golden brown, about 50 minutes. Remove from pans and cool on racks. Cover loosely with plastic wrap and let stand at least 2 hours. Slice thin and arrange on baking sheets. Toast in 250-degree oven, turning until golden brown, 1 hour or less. Cool on racks; store in airtight container.

SLICE & BAKE ZANTE CURRANT COOKIES

1 cup butter, softened
1 cup powdered sugar
½ cup sugar
1 egg
2 teaspoons vanilla
2½ cups flour
½ teaspoon baking soda
1 cup zante currants or chopped raisins

Combine butter, sugars, egg, and vanilla; beat until light and fluffy. In small bowl, combine flour and baking soda; stir into butter mixture and currants or raisins and mix well. Shape into 12-inch roll or two 8- to 10-inch rolls; cover in plastic wrap and chill until firm. Preheat oven to 350 degrees. Slice into ½-inch-thick slices; place on ungreased cookie sheets and bake 10 to 12 minutes. Makes 4 dozen.

BIRTHDAY CAKE FOR JESUS

1 chocolate cake mix
White frosting
Green tube frosting

Yellow tube frosting
Red candle

Make a 3-layer chocolate cake using one box of cake mix. Ice between layers and over entire cake with white frosting. Trim the top rim of the cake in the shape of a wreath with green frosting. Make a large star shape in the middle of the wreath with yellow frosting. Place red candle in the middle of the star.

Symbolism:
Round cake represents earth.
Three layers represent the Trinity (Father, Son, and Holy Spirit).
Chocolate represents sin in the world.
White icing represents our cleansed hearts.
One candle represents Jesus, the Light of the world.
Yellow star represents the light of the Wise Men.
The green wreath represents the new life we have in Jesus Christ.

CARROT CAKE

3 cups grated carrots
2 cups flour
1 cup oil
4 eggs
1 tablespoon baking powder
1 teaspoon baking soda
2 cups sugar
½ teaspoon salt

Preheat oven to 300 degrees. Mix together all ingredients by hand, then with electric mixer at medium-high speed for 3 minutes. Grease and flour 9x13-inch cake pan. Add mixture to pan and bake 30 to 45 minutes, or until toothpick inserted in center comes out clean.

ALMOND ROCHA

36 salted crackers
1 cup butter
1 cup brown sugar
½ cup chocolate chips
Ground almonds

Preheat oven to 350 degrees. Place crackers on cookie sheet. In a saucepan, melt butter and brown sugar over low heat. Slowly boil for 4 minutes, stirring constantly. Pour over crackers. Bake 8 minutes. Pour chocolate chips on top. Place back in oven for 2 to 3 minutes until melted. Spread chocolate out with a knife. Sprinkle almonds on top. Refrigerate and break apart when hard.

CHURCH WINDOWS

1 cup semisweet chocolate chips
2 tablespoons butter
1 egg, beaten
3 cups colored miniature marshmallows
1 cup pecans, chopped
Powdered sugar

In a saucepan, melt chocolate and butter over low heat. Remove from heat and add egg. Mix well. Cool slightly. Mix marshmallows and nuts in a large bowl. Pour chocolate mixture over marshmallows and nuts; mix well. Divide mixture in half. Sprinkle waxed paper with powdered sugar, roll around cookie mixture, and shape into a roll. Chill for several hours. Slice to serve.

CRISP PEPPERNUTS

1 cup butter, softened
1½ cups brown sugar
1 egg, beaten
2 tablespoons syrup
2 teaspoons soda

1 teaspoon cinnamon
1 teaspoon cloves
1 teaspoon ginger
1 teaspoon anise
3¼ cups flour

Cream butter and sugar. Add beaten egg and syrup. Add soda, spices, and anise. Mix well. Add flour; mix well. Let dough stand in refrigerator overnight. Preheat oven to 375 degrees. Take a small amount of dough and roll into a long "worm." Slice small peppernuts off and bake 5 to 10 minutes on cookie sheets.

INDEX